AFRAID

by Kerry Dinmont

The
Child's
World®
childsworld.com

Published by The Child's World®
1980 Lookout Drive • Mankato, MN 56003-1705
800-599-READ • www.childsworld.com

Photographs ©: Shutterstock Images, cover,
1, 4, 8, 13, 16, 22 (top right), 22 (bottom
left), 22 (bottom right); Ivonne Wierink/
Shutterstock Images, 5; Inna Ska/Shutterstock
Images, 6; iStockphoto, 9, 17; Africa Studio/
Shutterstock Images, 10; India Picture/
Shutterstock Images, 14; ESB Professional/
Shutterstock Images, 18; Monkey Business
Images/Shutterstock Images, 21; Hogan
Imaging/Shutterstock Images, 22 (top left)

Design Elements: Shutterstock Images

ISBN Hardcover: 9781503828025
ISBN Paperback: 9781622434626
LCCN: 2018944224

Printed in the United States of America
PAO2395

ABOUT THE AUTHOR

Kerry Dinmont is a children's book author who enjoys art and nature. She lives in Montana with her two Norwegian elkhounds.

CONTENTS

Chapter One

ANNIE IS AFRAID

Annie is going to her friend Diego's house. Her mom drives her there. There is a dog at Diego's door. The dog barks.

Annie does not like dogs. A dog bit her once. Diego lets the dog past the gate. The big dog barks at Annie. Annie's heart beats fast. She runs to the car. Annie is afraid.

Chapter Two

BEING AFRAID

Everyone gets afraid sometimes. People get afraid when they feel **unsafe**. Being up high might make people afraid. People could be afraid when someone is shouting at them.

9

Being afraid might make your heart beat quickly. You might **freeze**. You might want to run away. Your hands might get cold. You might sweat or shake.

It is okay to be afraid. Tell trusted adults if you are afraid. They can help keep you safe.

THINK ABOUT IT

What makes you afraid?

You might be **scared** of things that are not really harmful. Tell trusted adults if you want to **overcome** a fear. They have also gotten over fears.

Chapter Three

HELPING OTHERS

Sometimes other people are afraid. They might run away. They could cry. They might hide.

You might not be afraid of the same thing as your friend. But do not force them to get over a fear. Let them know it is okay to be afraid.

It is most important to be someone's friend.
Let them know they have someone to
count on. That can make people less afraid.

WHO IS AFRAID?

Can you tell who is afraid? Turn to page 24 for the answer.

GLOSSARY

freeze (FREEZ) To freeze means to suddenly stop moving. Someone who is afraid might freeze.

overcome (oh-vur-KUM) To overcome something means to no longer be under its control. You might want to try to overcome a fear.

scared (SKAYRD) To be scared is to be afraid of something. Being scared means that you are afraid.

unsafe (un-SAFE) To feel unsafe is to feel as if something might harm you. People become afraid because they feel unsafe.

TO LEARN MORE

Books

Dinmont, Kerry. **Dan's First Day of School: A Book about Emotions**. Mankato, MN: The Child's World, 2018.

Nilsen, Genevieve. **Afraid**. Minneapolis, MN: Jump!, Inc., 2018.

Seeger, Laura Vaccaro. **I Used to Be Afraid**. New York, NY: Roaring Brook Press, 2015.

Web Sites

Visit our Web site for links about being afraid:
childsworld.com/links

Note to Parents, Teachers, and Librarians: We routinely verify our Web links to make sure they are safe and active sites. So encourage your readers to check them out!

INDEX